FIRST 50
BAROQUE PIECES
YOU SHOULD PLAY ON GUITAR

Compiled and Edited by John Hill

ISBN 978-1-5400-6931-3

HAL•LEONARD®

Visit Hal Leonard Online at
www.halleonard.com

Contact Us:
Hal Leonard
7777 West Bluemound Road
Milwaukee, WI 53213
Email: info@halleonard.com

In Europe, contact:
Hal Leonard Europe Limited
42 Wigmore Street
Marylebone, London, W1U 2RN
Email: info@halleonardeurope.com

In Australia, contact:
Hal Leonard Australia Pty. Ltd.
4 Lentara Court
Cheltenham, Victoria, 3192 Australia
Email: info@halleonard.com.au

CONTENTS

INTRODUCTION

The 50 compositions selected for this book represent a broad range of music from some of the great Baroque composers of Europe—from the elegant simplicity of the music of Robert de Visée, to the complexity and intensity of the music of Johann Sebastian Bach. These selections are presented alphabetically by composer, and not based on the technical difficulty of the pieces. Students of the classical guitar will find pieces suitable for their level of proficiency in this collection.

The Baroque period of music is generally considered to include compositions written between the years 1600 and 1750. However, as with other historical periods, the start and end dates are approximations, and the transition from the preceding Renaissance period (1450 to 1600) was gradual. As cultural and social norms slowly changed, so did various art forms, including music.

The lute, although extremely popular and prominent during the earlier Renaissance period, grew in complexity and popularity during the Baroque period. It acquired more strings, which in part stimulated a growth in depth and complexity of music and technique, inspiring composers across Europe to compose for the instrument. It achieved its pinnacle of artistry through the works of Johann Sebastian Bach, Sylvius Leopold Weiss, Robert de Visée, and others.

The Baroque period also gave rise to the popularity of the guitar. This was a slightly smaller instrument than the modern classical guitar, typically with five courses (double strings). The tuning was similar to the modern-day guitar with the most pronounced exception being the fourth string, which was typically either an octave D higher, or double-strung with a lower D and upper D. The Baroque guitar was a versatile instrument with the ability to provide chordal accompaniment for voice and other instruments, yet also stood on its own as a solo instrument. In addition, the guitar was a relatively affordable instrument (compared to keyboards for instance), which also contributed to its ever-increasing popularity.

Ornamentation was an integral part of Baroque performance practice, whether the composer wrote out specific ornaments, or left this (in part, or entirely) up to the player. It was expected that the accomplished player would ornament the written notes with passing tones, trills, and other embellishments. In this collection, basic trills, passing tones, and other ornaments have been written into the music at points deemed appropriate. However, in the spirit of Baroque performance practice, the player should play these as indicated, modify them, or add additional Baroque ornamentation where appropriate.

Tempo (metronome) indications as we know them today did not exist during the Baroque period. During the 17th century, there was a gradual transition to the use of editorial adjectives as suggestions for the tempo of a particular piece of music. Many of these are familiar to the modern-day player—for example, *Adagio, Allegro,* and *Presto*. Other pieces had commonly used names that Baroque musicians understood to have certain performance requirements, such as *Menuet, Gigue*, and *Sarabande*. As with the application of ornamentation, much was left to the ability and taste of the performer. The metronome markings in this collection are *suggestions* for performance, and each piece could have a range of tempi according to the interpretation and proficiency of the player.

I hope you find the music in this collection rewarding and inspirational.

John Hill

BIOGRAPHY

John Hill is an accomplished guitarist and educator whose career spans over 30 years of performance, teaching, and publishing. He currently teaches at Concordia University, Mequon, WI. He received his undergraduate degree in Guitar Performance from the Guildhall School of Music and Drama in London, England, and his Masters of Music in Guitar Performance from Ithaca College, Ithaca, NY.

In addition to performance and teaching, John Hill has arranged and compiled numerous collections of classical guitar music for Hal Leonard, including:

Masterworks for Guitar • HL00699503

The Beatles for Classical Guitar • HL00699237

Christmas Songs for Classical Guitar • HL00701198

Disney Songs for Classical Guitar • HL00701753

Hymns for Classical Guitar • HL 00701898

Sacred Songs for Classical Guitar • HL00702426

Italian Songs for Classical Guitar • HL00701899

Classic Rock for Classical Guitar • HL00703633

Classical Guitar Christmas Sheet Music • HL00146974

First 50 Pieces You Should Play on Classical Guitar • HL00155414

Journey Through the Classics • HL00122489

The Great Arpeggios Book • HL00277252

Fugue
BWV 998

Johann Sebastian Bach
(1685-1750)

Tuning:
(low to high) D-A-D-G-B-E

(♩ = 63)

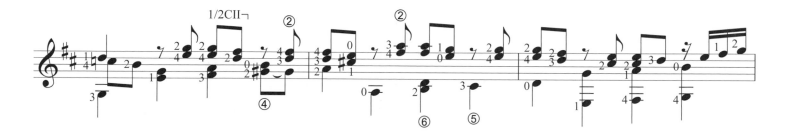

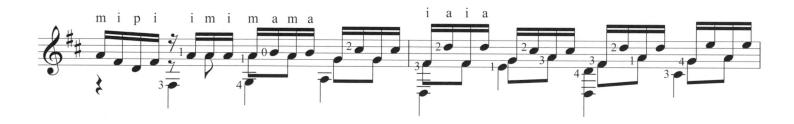

9

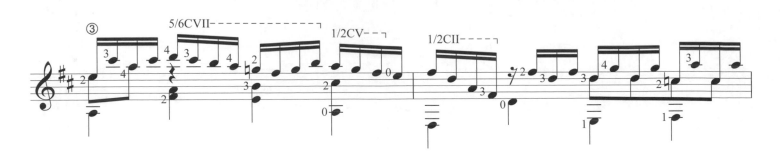

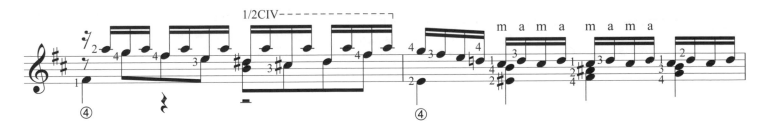

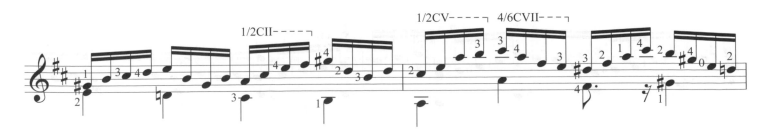

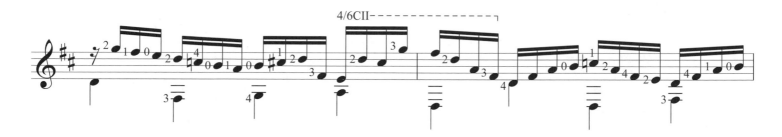

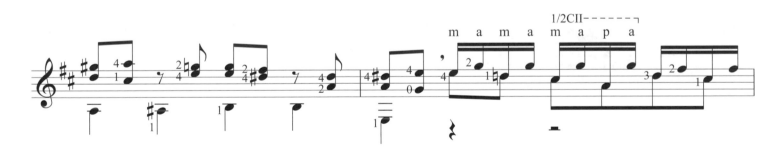

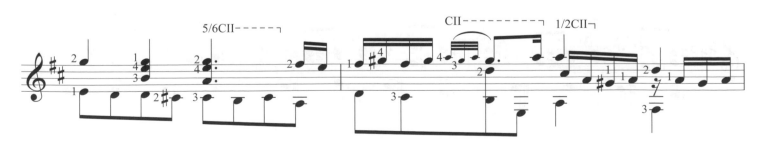

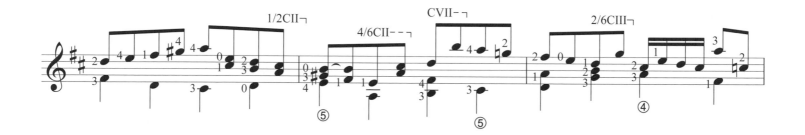

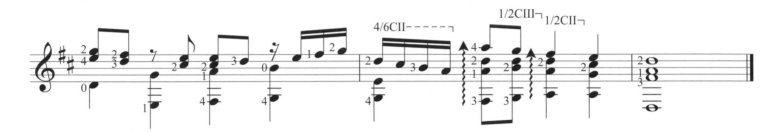

LUTE SUITE NO. 4, BWV 1006a
Prelude

Johann Sebastian Bach
(1685-1750)

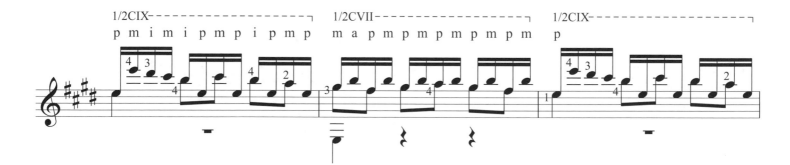

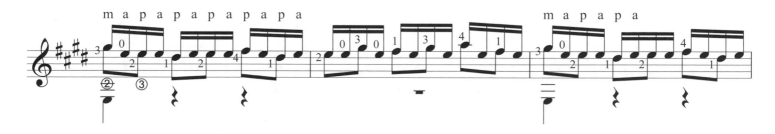

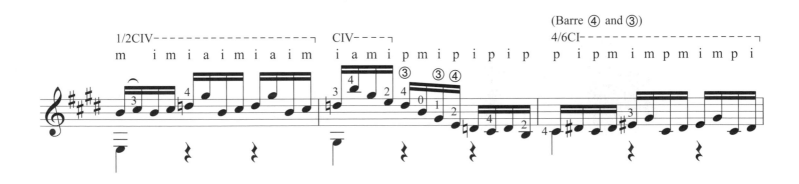

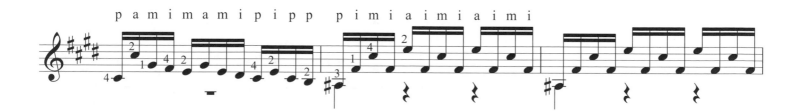

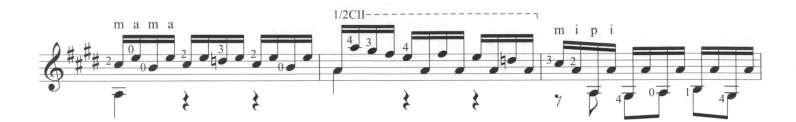

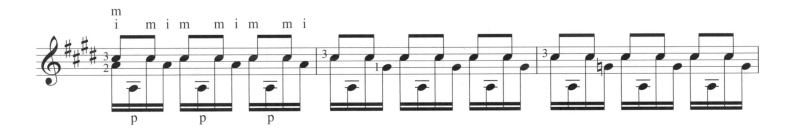

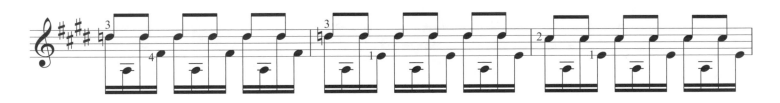

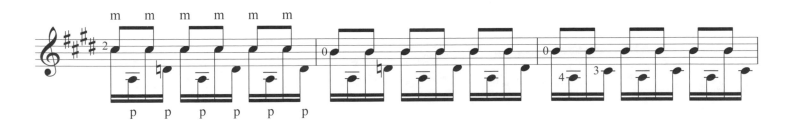

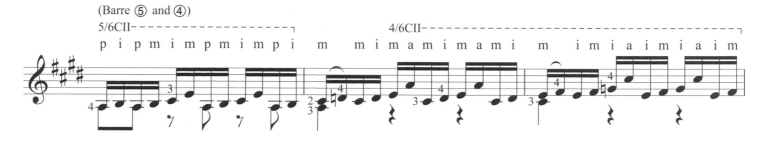

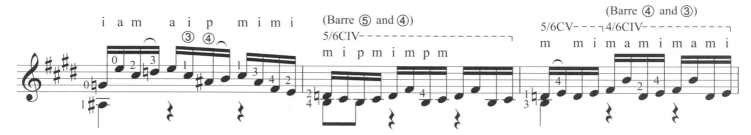

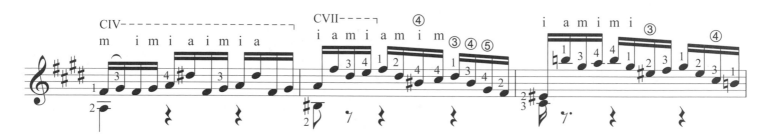

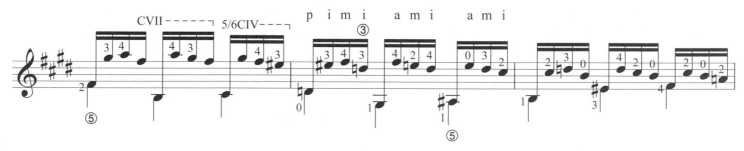

19

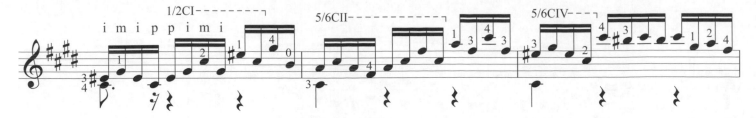

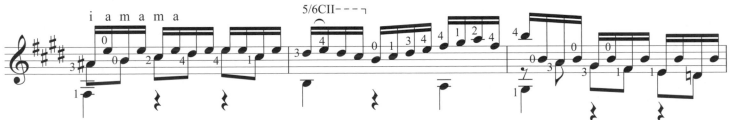

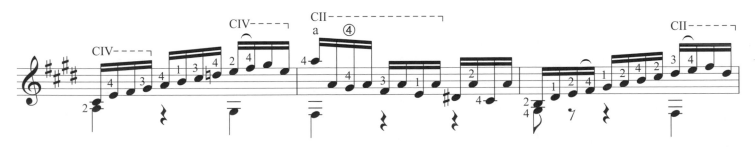

*Alternative:

20

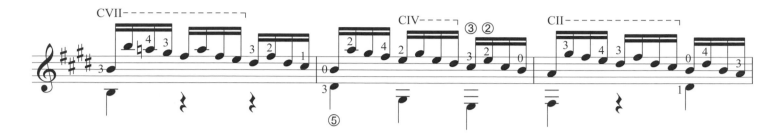

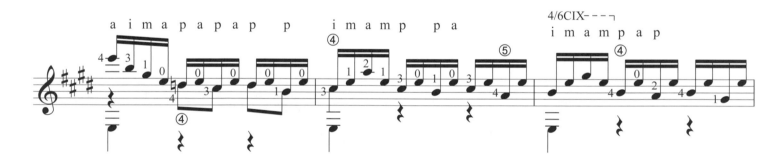

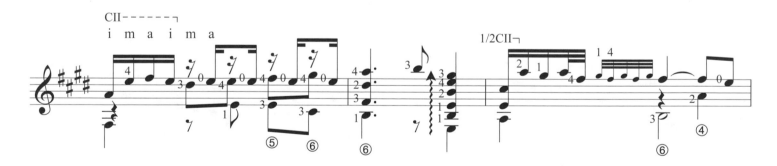

21

Loure

Johann Sebastian Bach
(1685-1750)

Gavotte en Rondeau

Johann Sebastian Bach
(1685-1750)

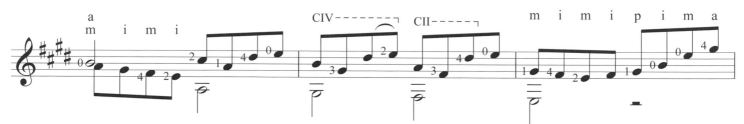

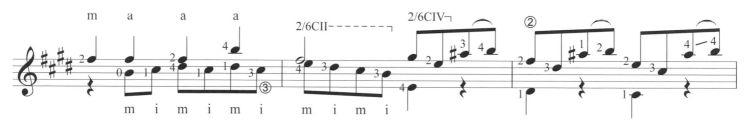

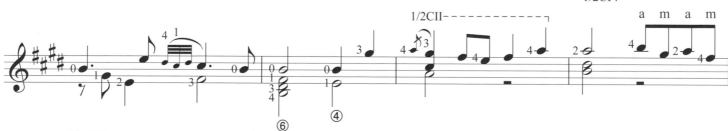

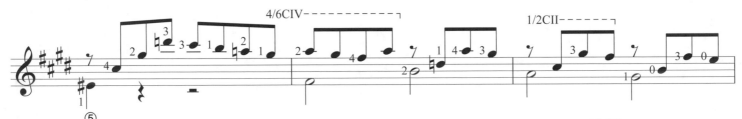
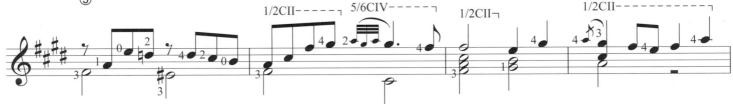
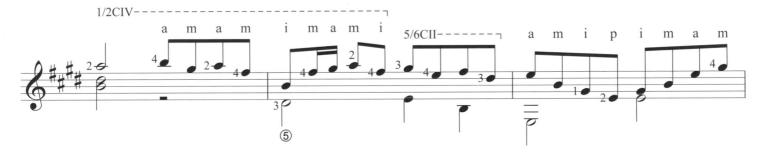

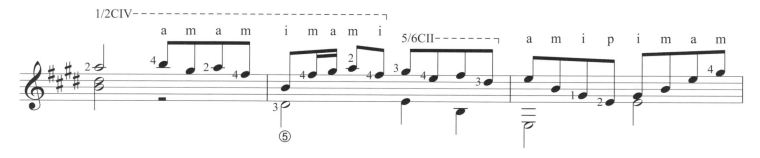

Menuet No. 1

Johann Sebastian Bach
(1685-1750)

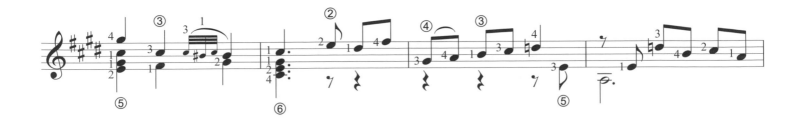

Menuet No. 2

Johann Sebastian Bach
(1685-1750)

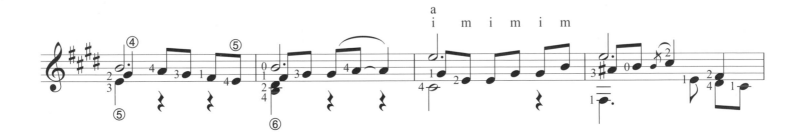

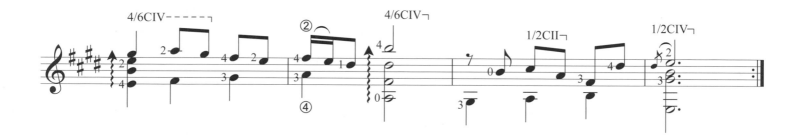

Bourée

Johann Sebastian Bach
(1685-1750)

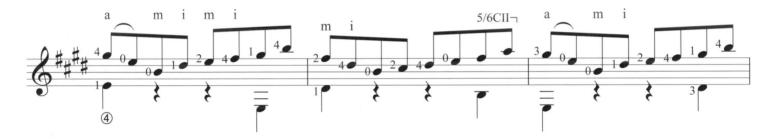

Gigue

Johann Sebastian Bach
(1685-1750)

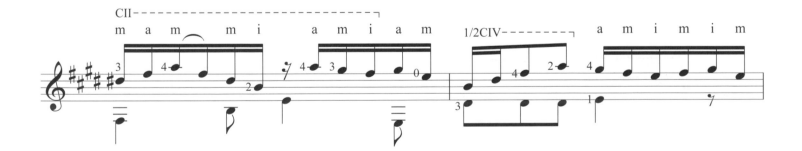

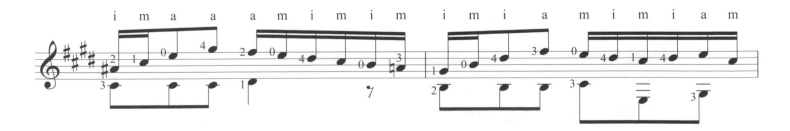

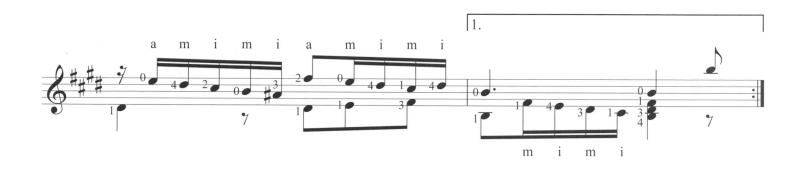

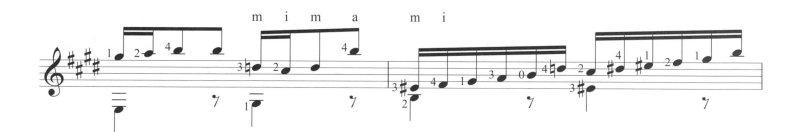

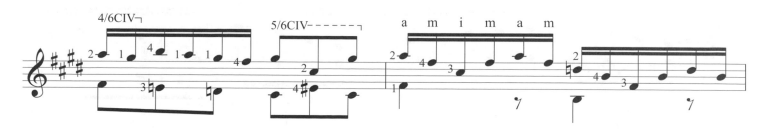

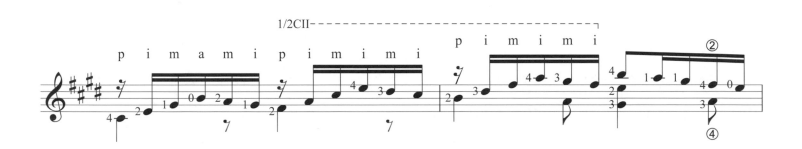

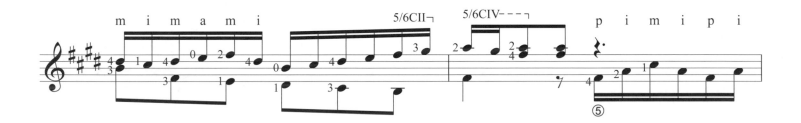

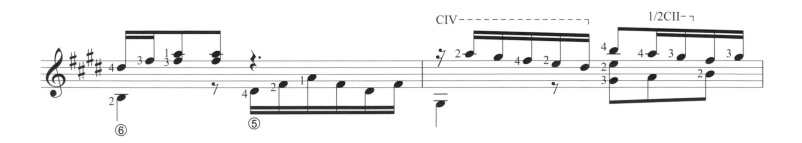

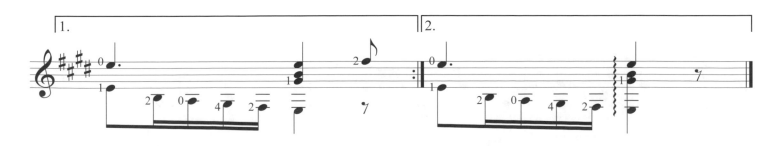

Bourée

Graf Bergen
(c. 1690-)

Sarabande
from PARTITA NO. 1 FOR VIOLIN

Johann Sebastian Bach
(1685-1750)
Arr. by John Hill

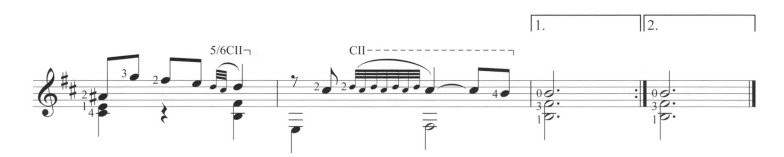

Courante

Ernst Gottlieb Baron
(1696-1760)

Menuet

Ernst Gottlieb Baron
(1696-1760)

Allegro

Santiago de Murcia
(1673-1739)

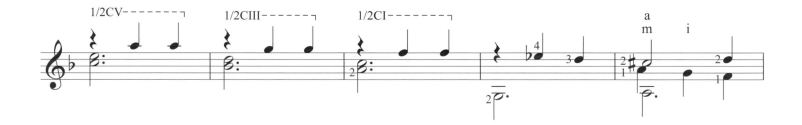

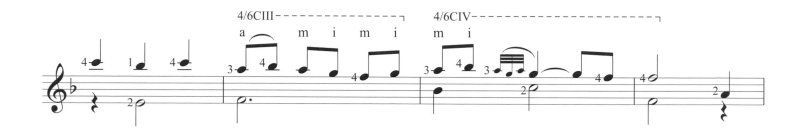

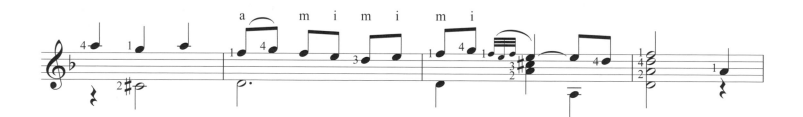

Prelude

Santiago de Murcia
(1673-1739)

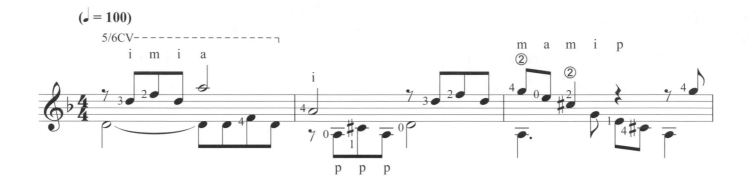

Tocata

Santiago de Murcia
(1673-1739)

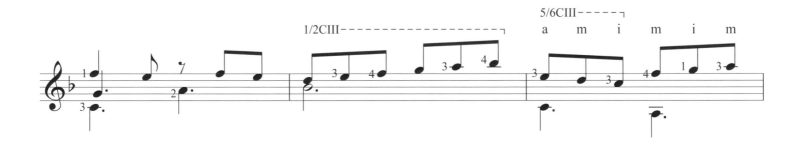

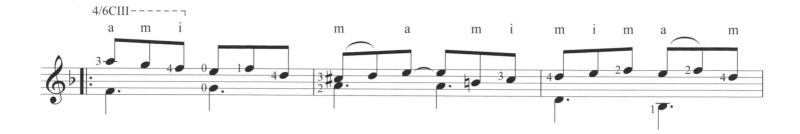

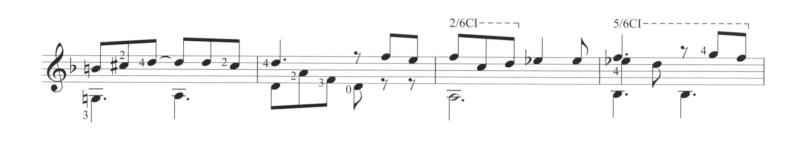

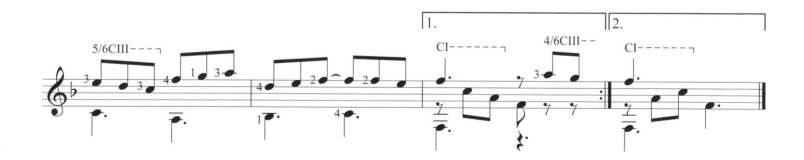

Masquarade

Robert de Visée
(c. 1655-c. 1732)

($\downarrow$ = 108)

50

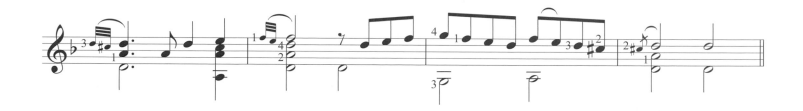

Menuet

Robert de Visée
(c. 1655-c. 1732)

Selections from
SUITE IN D MINOR
Prelude

Robert de Visée
(c. 1655-c. 1732)

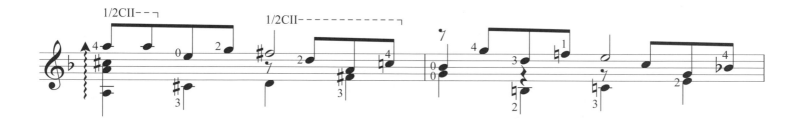

Allemande

Robert de Visée
(c. 1655-c. 1732)

$(\half = 60)$

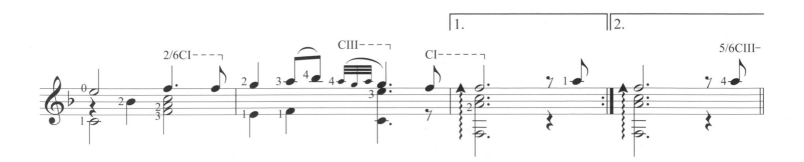

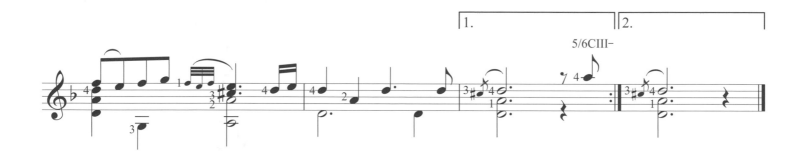

Courante

Robert de Visée
(c. 1655-c. 1732)

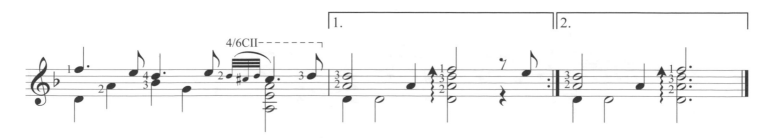

Sarabande

Robert de Visée
(c. 1655-c. 1732)

Gavotte

Robert de Visée
(c. 1655-c. 1732)

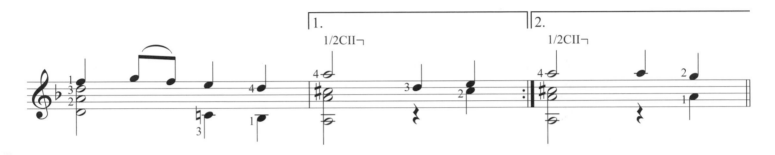

Bourée

Robert de Visée
(c. 1655-c. 1732)

Gigue

Robert de Visée
(c. 1655-c. 1732)

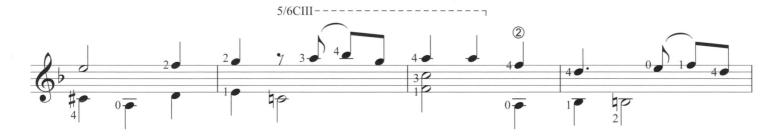

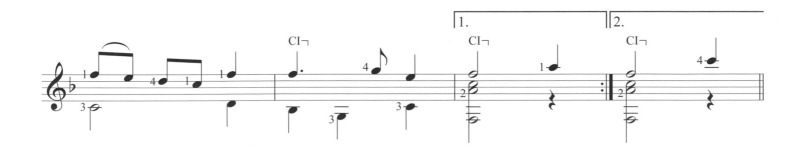

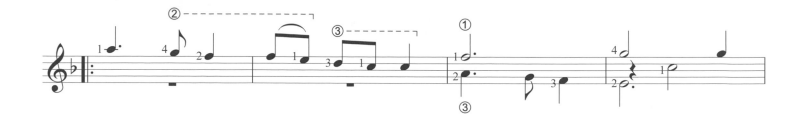

Bourée

Jacques de Saint Luc
(1616-c. 1710)

Gavotte

Johann Fischer
(c. 1656-1746)

Menuet

Johann Philipp Krieger
(1649-1725)

Gigue

Jan Antonín Losy
(c. 1650-1721)

Menuet

Jan Antonín Losy
(c. 1650-1721)

Almain

Henry Purcell
(c. 1659-1695)
Arr. by John Hill

Tuning:
(low to high) D-A-D-G-B-E

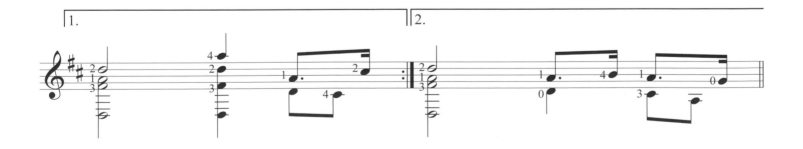

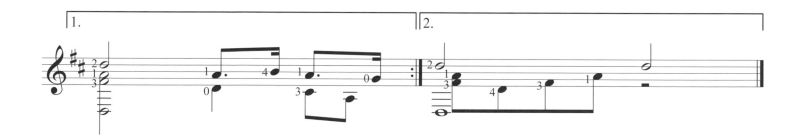

Borry

Henry Purcell
(c. 1659-1695)
Arr. by John Hill

Menuet

Henry Purcell
(c. 1659-1695)
Arr. by John Hill

Trumpet Tune

Henry Purcell
(c. 1659-1695)
Arr. by John Hill

Tuning:
(low to high) D-A-D-G-B-E

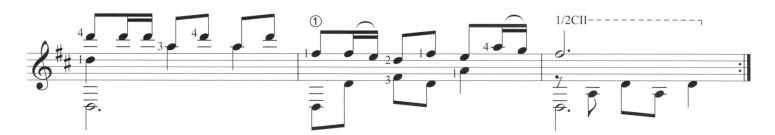

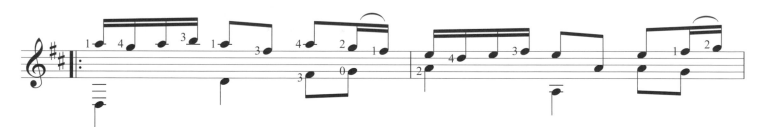

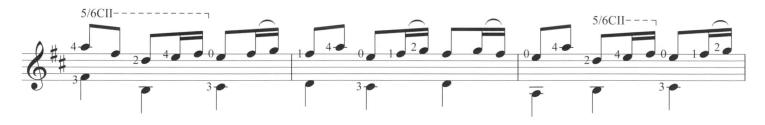

Sarabande

Ludovico Roncalli
(1654-1713)

Aria

Johann Sigismund Scholze
(1705-1750)

Canarios

Gaspar Sanz
(1640-1710)

Tuning:
(low to high) D-A-D-G-B-E

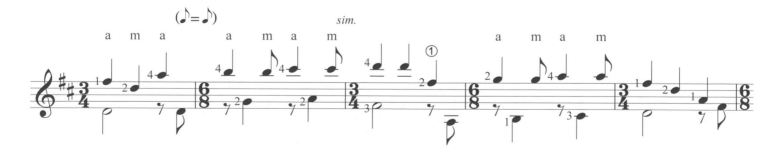

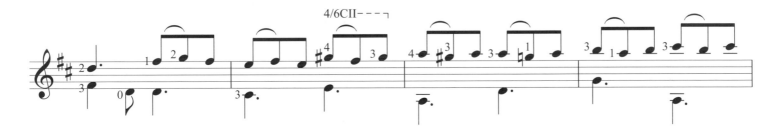

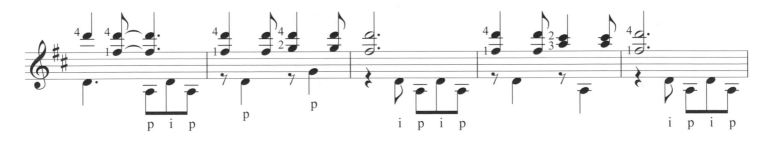

76

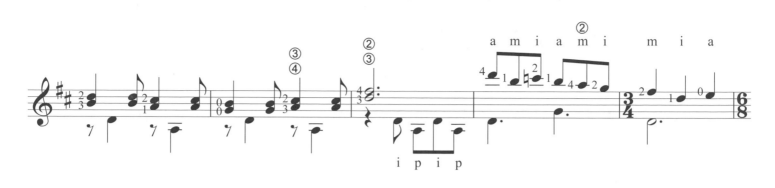

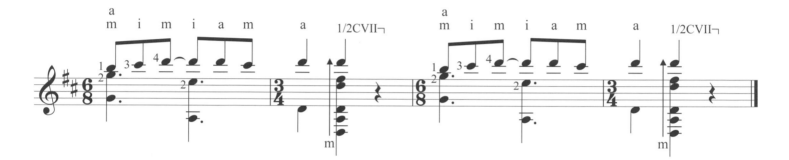

La Caballería de Nápoles
con Dos Clarines
(The Cavalry of Naples with Two Bugles)

Gaspar Sanz
(1640-1710)

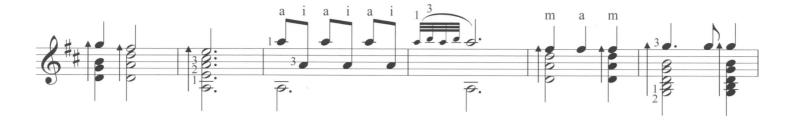

Marizapalos

Gaspar Sanz
(1640-1710)

Pavana

Gaspar Sanz
(1640-1710)

poco rit.

a tempo

1/2CV- - - - - - - - - - - - - - - - - -

1/2CV¬

⑤

1/2CV¬

⑤   pont.   ⑤

Villanos

Gaspar Sanz
(1640-1710)

TRIO SONATA, RV 82
Allegro Non Molto

Antonio Vivaldi
(1678-1741)

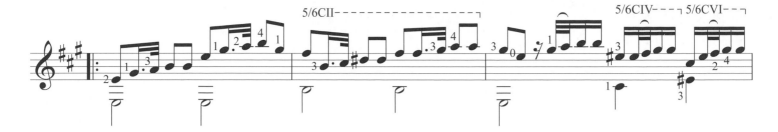

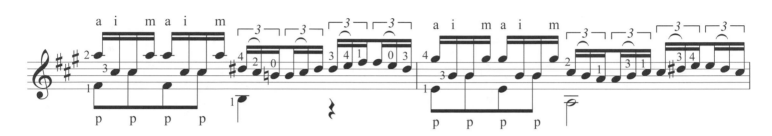

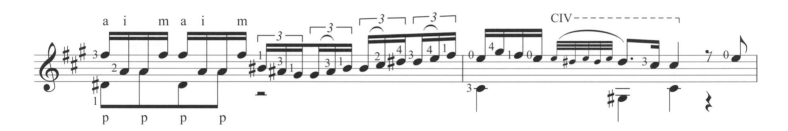

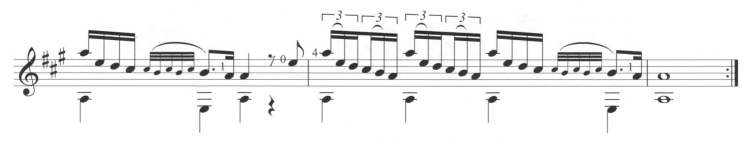

Larghetto

Antonio Vivaldi
(1678-1741)

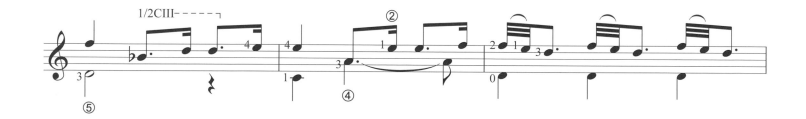

Allegro

Antonio Vivaldi
(1678-1741)

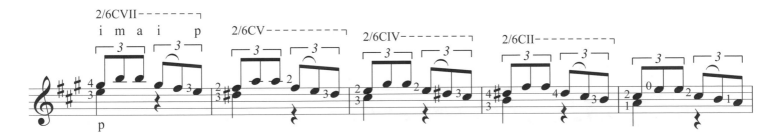

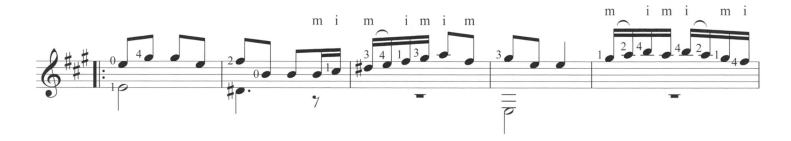

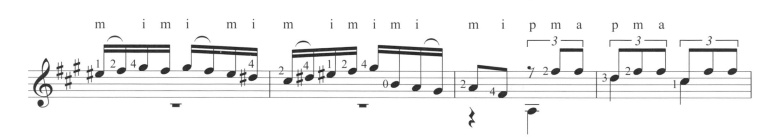

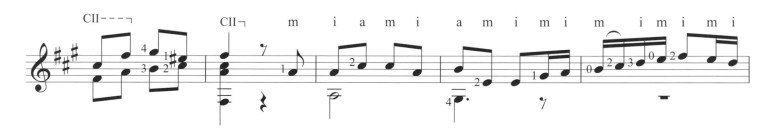

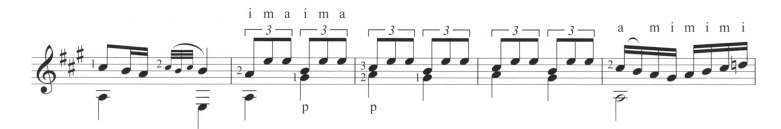

Sonata
K. 11

Domenico Scarlatti
(1685-1757)
Arr. by John Hill

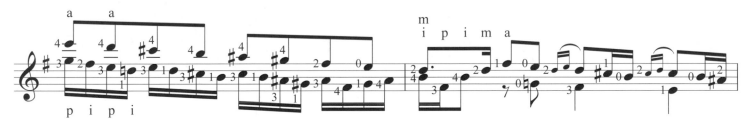

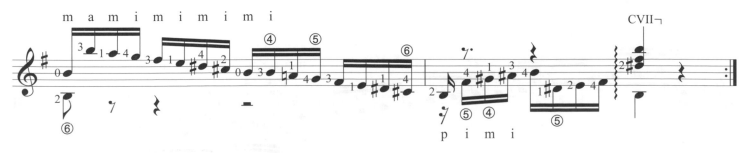

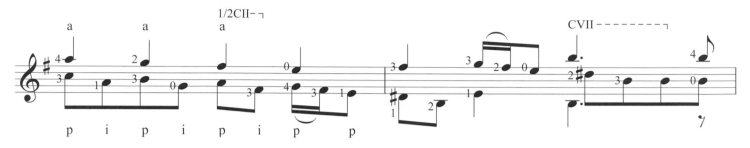

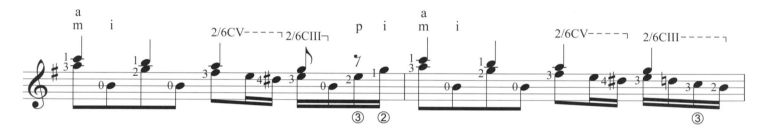
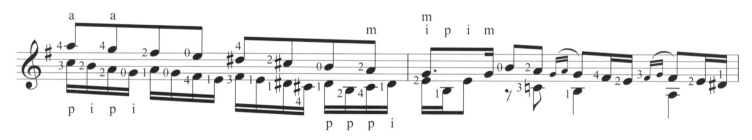

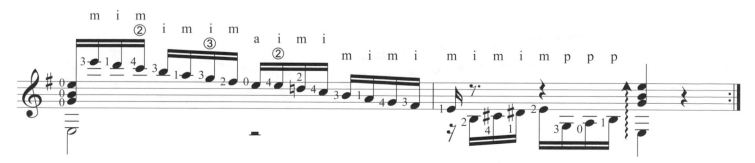

Sonata
K. 322

Domenico Scarlatti
(1685-1757)
Arr. by John Hill

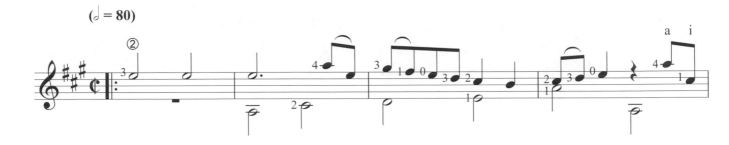

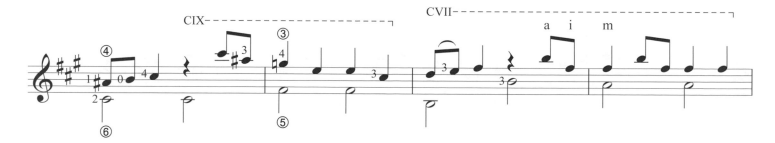

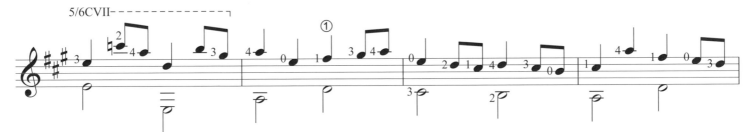

Fantasie

Sylvius Leopold Weiss
(1687-1750)

Tuning:
(low to high) D-A-D-G-B-E

Note: In keeping with the original lute manuscript, barlines have been left
out of the first section of this *Fantasie* to denote freedom of expression.

(♩ = 58)

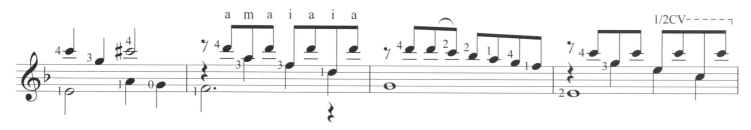

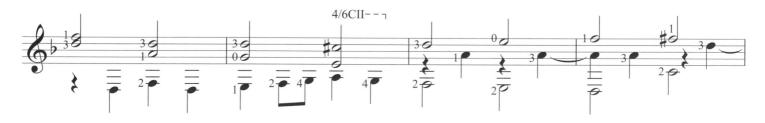

Passacaglia

Sylvius Leopold Weiss
(1687-1750)

Tuning:
(low to high) D-A-D-G-B-E

($\downarrow$ = 63)

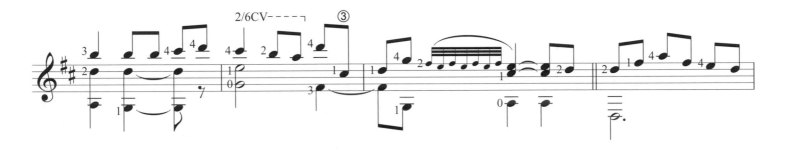

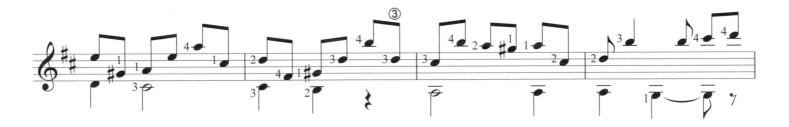

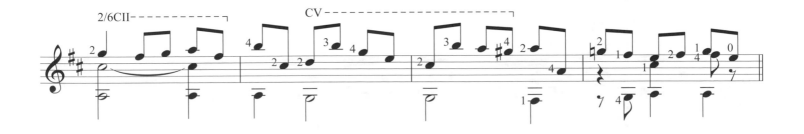

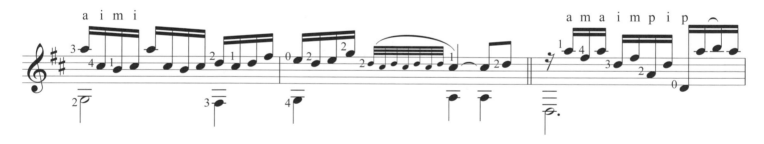

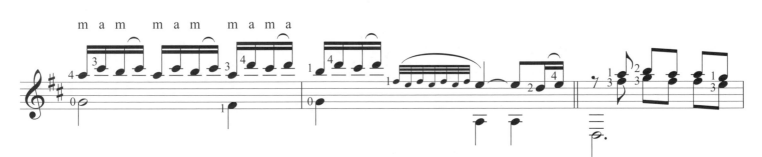

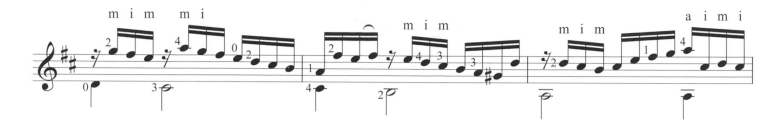

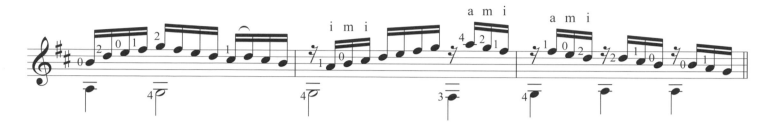

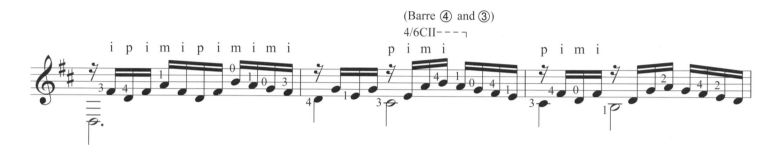

Paysane

from SUITE NO. 25, L'INFIDELE

Sylvius Leopold Weiss
(1687-1750)

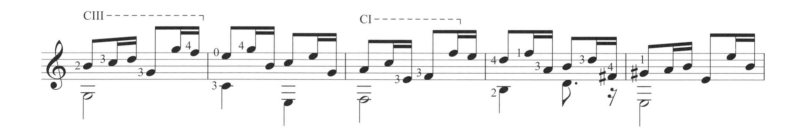

Prelude

Sylvius Leopold Weiss
(1687-1750)

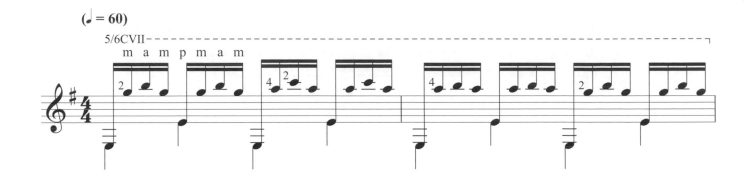

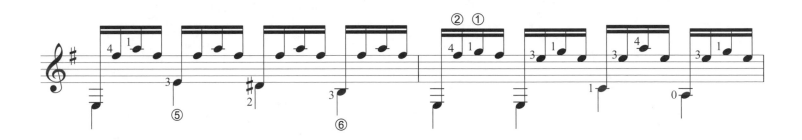

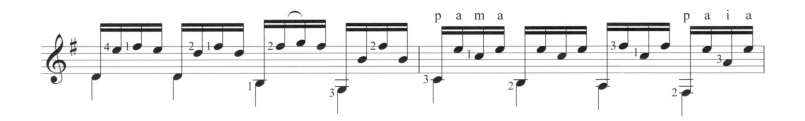

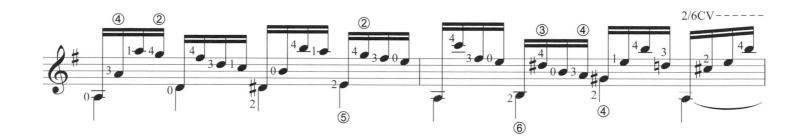

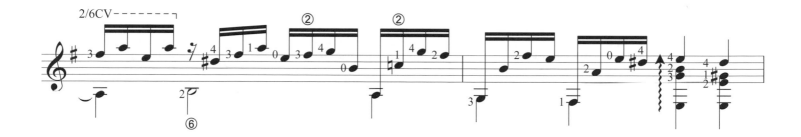

Prelude
from SUITE NO. 4

Sylvius Leopold Weiss
(1687-1750)

Note: In keeping with the original lute manuscript, barlines have been left out of this *Prelude* to denote freedom of expression.

CLASSICAL GUITAR

PUBLICATIONS FROM HAL LEONARD

THE BEATLES FOR CLASSICAL GUITAR

Includes 20 solos from big Beatles hits arranged for classical guitar, complete with left-hand and right-hand fingering. Songs include: All My Loving • And I Love Her • Can't Buy Me Love • Fool on the Hill • From a Window • Hey Jude • If I Fell • Let It Be • Michelle • Norwegian Wood • Obla Di • Ticket to Ride • Yesterday • and more. Features arrangements and an introduction by Joe Washington, as well as his helpful hints on classical technique and detailed notes on how to play each song. The book also covers parts and specifications of the classical guitar, tuning, and Joe's "Strata System" – an easy-reading system applied to chord diagrams.

00699237 Classical Guitar $19.99

CZERNY FOR GUITAR

INCLUDES TAB

12 SCALE STUDIES FOR CLASSICAL GUITAR

by David Patterson

Adapted from Carl Czerny's *School of Velocity, Op. 299* for piano, this lesson book explores 12 keys with 12 different approaches or "treatments." You will explore a variety of articulations, ranges and technical perspectives as you learn each key. These arrangements will not only improve your ability to play scales fluently, but will also develop your ears, knowledge of the fingerboard, reading abilities, strength and endurance. In standard notation and tablature.

00701248 ....$9.99

MATTEO CARCASSI – 25 MELODIC AND PROGRESSIVE STUDIES, OP. 60

arr. Paul Henry

One of Carcassi's (1792-1853) most famous collections of classical guitar music – indispensable for the modern guitarist's musical and technical development. Performed by Paul Henry. 49-minute audio accompaniment.

00696506 Book/Online Audio $17.99

CLASSICAL & FINGERSTYLE GUITAR TECHNIQUES

INCLUDES TAB

by David Oakes • Musicians Institute

This Master Class is aimed at any electric or acoustic guitarist who wants a quick, thorough grounding in the essentials of classical and fingerstyle technique. Topics covered include: arpeggios and scales, free stroke and rest stroke, P-i scale technique, three-to-a-string patterns, natural and artificial harmonics, tremolo and rasgueado, and more. The book includes 12 intensive lessons for right and left hand in standard notation & tab, and the audio features 92 solo acoustic tracks.

00695171 Book/Online Audio $17.99

CLASSICAL GUITAR CHRISTMAS COLLECTION

INCLUDES TAB

Includes classical guitar arrangements in standard notation and tablature for more than two dozen beloved carols: Angels We Have Heard on High • Auld Lang Syne • Ave Maria • Away in a Manger • Canon in D • The First Noel • God Rest Ye Merry, Gentlemen • Hark! the Herald Angels Sing • I Saw Three Ships • Jesu, Joy of Man's Desiring • Joy to the World • O Christmas Tree • O Holy Night • Silent Night • What Child Is This? • and more.

00699493 Guitar Solo $10.99

CLASSICAL GUITAR WEDDING

INCLUDES TAB

Perfect for players hired to perform for someone's big day, this songbook features 16 classical wedding favorites arranged for solo guitar in standard notation and tablature. Includes: Air on the G String • Ave Maria • Bridal Chorus • Canon in D • Jesu, Joy of Man's Desiring • Minuet • Sheep May Safely Graze • Wedding March • and more.

00699563 Solo Guitar with Tab.............................$12.99

CLASSICAL MASTERPIECES FOR GUITAR

INCLUDES TAB

27 works by Bach, Beethoven, Handel, Mendelssohn, Mozart and more transcribed with standard notation and tablature. Now anyone can enjoy classical material regardless of their guitar background. Also features stay-open binding.

00699312 ....$14.99

MASTERWORKS FOR GUITAR

INCLUDES TAB

Over 60 Favorites from Four Centuries
World's Great Classical Music

Dozens of classical masterpieces: Allemande • Bourree • Canon in D • Jesu, Joy of Man's Desiring • Lagrima • Malaguena • Mazurka • Piano Sonata No. 14 in C# Minor (Moonlight) Op. 27 No. 2 First Movement Theme • Ode to Joy • Prelude No. I (Well-Tempered Clavier).

00699503 ....$19.99

A MODERN APPROACH TO CLASSICAL GUITAR

by Charles Duncan

This multi-volume method was developed to allow students to study the art of classical guitar within a new, more contemporary framework. For private, class or self-instruction. Book One incorporates chord frames and symbols, as well as a recording to assist in tuning and to provide accompaniments for at-home practice. Book One also introduces beginning fingerboard technique and music theory. Book Two and Three build upon the techniques learned in Book One.

00695114 Book 1 – Book Only $6.99
00695113 Book 1 – Book/Online Audio...............$10.99
00695116 Book 2 – Book Only $6.99
00695115 Book 2 – Book/Online Audio...............$10.99
00699202 Book 3 – Book Only $9.99
00695117 Book 3 – Book/Online Audio...............$12.99
00695119 Composite Book/CD Pack $29.99

ANDRES SEGOVIA – 20 STUDIES FOR GUITAR

Sor/Segovia

20 studies for the classical guitar written by Beethoven's contemporary, Fernando Sor, revised, edited and fingered by the great classical guitarist Andres Segovia. These essential repertoire pieces continue to be used by teachers and students to build solid classical technique. Features 50-minute demonstration audio.

00695012 Book/Online Audio $19.99
00006363 Book Only...$7.99

THE FRANCISCO COLLECTION TÁRREGA

INCLUDES TAB

edited and performed by Paul Henry

Considered the father of modern classical guitar, Francisco Tárrega revolutionized guitar technique and composed a wealth of music that will be a cornerstone of classical guitar repertoire for centuries to come. This unique book/audio pack features 14 of his most outstanding pieces in standard notation and tab, edited and performed by virtuoso Paul Henry. Includes: Adelita • Capricho Árabe • Estudio Brillante • Grand Jota • Lágrima • Malagueña • María • Recuerdos de la Alhambra • Tango • and more, plus bios of Tárrega and Henry.

00698993 Book/Online Audio $19.99

HAL•LEONARD®

Visit Hal Leonard Online at **www.halleonard.com**

Prices, contents and availability subject to change without notice.